Linn County Leg-Breaker

Poems by K.W. Peery

Spartan
Press

Spartan Press

Kansas City, MO
spartanpresskc.com

Spartan
Press

Copyright © Kevin Peery, 2021
First Edition: 1 3 5 7 9 10 8 6 4 2
ISBN: 978-1-952411-68-7
LCCN: 2021943647

Cover image: Kevin Peery
Author photo: Kevin Peery

Spartan Press titles by K.W. Peery:

Linn County Leg-Breaker (2021)

Hellraiser's Hieroglyphics (2019)

Hillbilly Hand Grenades (2019)

Bootleggers Bluff (2018)

Table of Contents

Linn County Leg-Breaker

Well I was born a rambler friends,
      and I intend to die that way.
It could be twenty years from now
      it could be most any day.
But if there ain't no whiskey and women
      lord behind those heavenly doors,
I'm gonna take my chances down below
      and of that you can be sure.

-Townes Van Zandt

For my friend and hero.

Billy Joe Shaver ~

August 16, 1939 - October 28, 2020

HELLCAT

When Hellcat
was on Hospice
she made me
promise to
take her ashes
up to Lassen Peak
the next August
and scatter them
at Lake Helen
because the
devil couldn't
find her
there

SOUTHPAW SOLUTION

We were
squared off
in the gravel
parkin' lot
just East of
Friendly Tavern

When I heard
ole Joe say -
'Ya better
watch that sneaky
son of a bitch...
He's a
southpaw'

So I
immediately
switched stances
and invited the
big bastard
in a little
closer

So I
could apply
my signature
chokehold

and get back to
shootin' eight ball
before the
bartender cried
last call

WIN WITHOUT 'EM KNOWIN'

Uncle Don
used to say -
'If you
don't like
what's bein'
said...
then find
a unique way
to change the
conversation' –

So I did -

And I do -

N' so
should
you -

If the
truth gets
twisted up
so much
there's
no other way
to win
without 'em
knowin'

EIGHT ELECTRIFYING MINUTES

In the
late night
HBO glow
of our
19 inch
Chromacolor
Zenith

I watched
Marvelous
Marvin Hagler
defend his
undisputed
middleweight titles
against Thomas
'The Hitman'
Hearns

It was
eight of
the most
electrifying
minutes
an eleven
year old
country boy
could possibly
witness

N'
how in
the hell
did a fight
so short
have such
a lasting
impact
on me
for more than
thirty-three
years

I guess
it's the
relentless
intensity
I witnessed
that night
in April of
Eighty-Five

When
two men
went to war
with one another
knowin' full well
no ringside bell
could save
them

SOUL SHATTERED HALO

The
switchgrass
was splattered
with bloody
bone fragments
and jellified
gray matter

And
there were
dime-sized tufts
of his distinguished
silver hairline
peakin' out
from the
congealed
purple pool

In a
soul
shattered
halo
where his
third eye
used to be

ONE LAST TANGO

After
a half dozen
dirty vodka martinis
at Doppelganger bar
in Buenos Aires

I slithered
my way
down Caminito
for one
last tango
with the
Lady in Red

SIDESWIPED LINCOLN

It was
a two for one
well drink
Sunday night
at Mongo's Planet
in Memphis

When I
sideswiped
Cybill Shepherd's
eighty-eight
Lincoln
Continental

And
to my
inebriated
surprise...
she wasn't
really
all that
pissed

Cybill just
asked me
to give her
a lift

to this
brand new
crib she'd
built off
Magnolia
Mound Drive

Where I
spent the
rest of that
full moon
night
poolside

Because
Cybill was
convinced
I'd never
make it
back to
Millington
in a Dodge
Dakota
with the side
caved in

DEADBOLT'S DEBT

Three days
before
my friend
Deadbolt
drowned
in Lake
Killarney

He
told me
how much juice
he still owed
Shotgun Vinny
Cammarata

And said
there was
no easy way
a hillbilly hustler
like him
could turn
the worm
fast enough
to repay it

So instead
of playin'
snitch -

Deadbolt
just flipped
the script –

N' wacked
himself
before
anyone
from
St. Louis
could
find him

WARD 20

(For James Edward Deeds)

Uncle Sal
said he
could hear
an unsettled
spirit screamin'
down the
abandoned
West wing
of Ward 20
in Lunatic
Asylum
No. 3

And
thought
the ghost
was likely
Ozark Missouri
folk artist
James Edward
Deeds

Still searchin'
for a
hand-stitched
leather bound

portfolio
someone stole
from him
seventeen
years before
the earthworms
found him

MAGNIFICENT RUMBLE

Ronald's
seventy-eight
Electra Glide
made the most
magnificent
rumble

As he
eased down
East Crandall
like a
high plains
drifter
still thirsty
for revenge

HUNG

This jury
is hung
eleven
to one
and
I know
·they all
think
I'm guilty

TAIL GUNNER TOM

I could smell
Pappy's
wing grease
driftin' down
Messanie Street
to greet me
that hot
August
afternoon

Ya see -
We'd
just buried
ole tail gunner
Tom
three hours
before

And I
could hear
Faron
singin'
'Hello Walls'
through the
sweaty side door
as I wiped
more tears
away

UNCLE JOE'S

We were haulin'
a heavy load
of Ozark wildcat
out East
last November

When Peeve
spotted a sign
that said
Uncle Joe's
BBQ
Exit 83

So we
clocked
our stop
while makin'
the drop
in Ina

Then
feasted
on pulled pork
n' brisket
before hittin'
the road

To deliver
the rest
of our
Thanksgivin'
load
just eight
miles shy
of Louisville

THE HERD

It's
goddamn funny
how this
sick ass scene
of part time scribes
wants to push their
impotent agendas
citing violations
from an imaginary
rulebook

Preachin'
the gospel
according
to those
who are
somehow
still in love
with the sound
of their own
voices

Standin' tall
on that
gatekeeper's
soapbox
in an

empty room
hundreds
of miles away
from anything
truly meaningful
or disruptive

Echoin'
the same
ole shit
that's been
said a
thousand
times better
a million
times before

Pretendin'
too hard
to be the
genuine article
makes most
authentic
assholes
and just
the kind
of toothless
starvin' artists
the herd
has groomed
them to be

FRENCHY'S ON FRIDAY

I
would
get
my
high
fade
freshened
at
Frenchy's
every
Friday
afternoon

Then
slow
troll
down
Easley
Street

Just
to
see
which
sharks
had
already

stashed
their
getaway
cars
behind
the
shaker
joint
adjacent
to
The
Haystack

BIVOUAC JACK

Bivouac Jack
had an old
English bulldog
named Archibald
that wore
steampunk
aviator goggles
and rode shotgun
in his custom
chopper sidecar

And they made
that crooked leg
from Taos
to Sturgis
every August
for six
straight
years

Until Archie
got too sick
to travel
and Jack
wouldn't
dream
of leavin'
New Mexico
without
him

DOPE SICK

I was
dope sick
for a week
down in
Waco
with a
trunkload
of stolen
semi-autos
and enough
goddamn
ammo
to reclaim
the Alamo
once my
generic
Clonidine
kicked in

SOUNDTRACK SAL

When
they
finally
discovered
the
skeletal
remains
of
'Soundtrack
Sal'
he
was
loosely
chained
to
a
rusted
floor
drain
in
a
dope
den
off
Hickory
Street
in

the
West
Bottoms

And
when
some
of
the
local
news
crews
suspected
it
was
'Tony
Ripe'...

I
knew
their
twisted
theory
could
never
be
right

Because
I

saw
Willie's
muzzle
flash
twice
on
Cliff
Drive
that
warm
September
night
and
still
have
the
spent
brass
to
prove
it

OG MIKE

OG Mike
was 70
years old
when he
got pinched
with 32
grams of
black tar
heroin
stashed
in the
glove
compartment
of his
86 Cutlass
Supreme
off Van Brunt
and Bonita Street

Now
at 73...
he'll do
another
14...
on top of
the 9
he spent

locked up
down
in Potosi
for that
botched
bank job
in Jasper

Which
would've
been
his 56th
payday
over an
8 year
span...

but fate's
right hand
landed
and he's
been livin'
in a goddamn
nightmare
ever since

MEANER SWELLS

In four
more days
I'll be
forced
to embrace
forty-six

And
just like
the first
forty-five

I'm
gonna ride
the wickedest
ass waves
I can find

All the way
through
whichever
glorious gate
promises me
meaner swells
in the
next
life

SIX GUN

I dug three
hollow point
mushrooms
out of the wall
behind a
shuffleboard table
at Gunny's Mill
before the
Greene County
Sheriff's deputies
arrived

And despite
my best efforts
to recover all five
with a William Henry
spearpoint knife

Nothin' could
change the fact
that Knothead
was still
graveyard
dead

N' we'd
play hell
protectin'
ole Six Gun
because two
hot rounds
never found
an exit

CYCLONE JONES

Cyclone
Jones
was
also
known
as
the
Camden
County
Madman

And
while
I
only
saw
him
fight
twice
back
in
the
early
80s

He's
still
considered
the

most
infamous
Boothill
brawler
to
ever
bare
knuckle

After
his
dominant
hand
got
mangled
in
a
Minneapolis
Moline
corn
picker
and
the
southpaw
stance
was
all
he
had
left
to
offer

MONDAY MORNIN' MADNESS

This
Monday
mornin'
madness
feels
like
another
winnerless
race
with
a
shapeshiftin'
face

Drivin'
fifteen
over
in
an
airport
rental
on
bald
Goodyear
tires

Towards

a

blood

red

oblivion

that's

impossible

to

explain

BUSTER'S BLUES

When
I went
to visit
Buster
for the
final time
back in 93

He'd been
a bilateral
below
the knee
amputee
for about
sixteen
weeks

So
we just
sat there
in that
dimly lit
menthol
scented
livin' room

While he
told me
stories
about
Willie
Dixon
And
how the
'West Coast Blues'
by Wes Montgomery
was still
his favorite
song

MOOSE

Verse I

Well Grandpa
drove trucks
for forty five
years
n' could
two way
chatter
like an
auctioneer

Drove
millions
of miles
for that
Churchill
watch
and there
was nobody
smoother
when avoidin'
the cops –

CHORUS –

Yeah -
all the
gearjammers
just called him
Moose

He loved
long legged
women
and eighty
proof

Detroit...
Dallas...
or Muskogee
straight through

Yeah-
every
gearjammer
called him
Moose
Cause
all the
gearjammers
knew ole
Moose

Verse II

Well Grandpa
dressed better
than a
Sunday
preacher
with slicked
back hair
and military
creases

Carried
a fat
stack of
cash
n' thirty eight
Smith
and folks
round here
never fucked
with him

REPEAT CHORUS - (Twice)

EXECUTIN' EVIL

There's a
burn barrel
smolderin'
in my
backyard

Filled
with bone
fragments
of past
enemies

Too
goddamn
stupid
to realize
I had them
dead to
rights

N' they
never
dreamed
I'd be the
one comin'
to turn out
their lights

In the
middle
of a
humid ass
Summer
night

As every
shocked
expression
burned
the same

While I
stole their
emtpy souls
and fed
them
to the
flames

Ya know
executin' evil
seldom
comes
easy

But it's
always
somehow
worth it
in the
end

SUFFERIN' SOULS

(For Kenny)

We sat there
on Kenny's
boat dock
at Lake
Lotawana

Smokin' sticky
purple punch
while listenin' to
'A Band Called Bud'
by Blue Mountain

Tryin' to recall
all the
crooked lines
from 'She Wants
Me To Change'

Feelin'
a little less
deranged
fourteen
years later

Knowin' our
sufferin' souls
are damn
near ready
to be purged
Under the Stairs
once again

AFTERLIFE

Tom needs
to know
Now so
do I...
Can I
take this
all with me
In the
afterlife...
Oh...
Take it
all with me...
In the
afterlife –

I'm
just a
three legged
hound
On a
cobblestone
street...
With a
t-bone steak
And two
left feet...

Ole Tom's
still pacin'
Along
Johnny's
white
lines...
Just
waitin'
on Roy
To
thumb
a ride

Yeah...
Waitin'
on Roy
In the
afterlife

Cause
I'm
stoned
here
waitin'
On the
afterlife

CENTRAL STONE

(For Uncle Chap)

I would
just sit
there alone
in the
Central Stone
scale house

Listenin' to
Paul Harvey
pontificate
over the
smooth blue
vibrations
of a worn out
window unit

Just waitin'
to watch
Uncle Chap
arm wrestle
an ole rebuilt
922B...
through a
caked n'
corroded
limestone
screen

Yeah...
Uncle Charlie
always said –

'This new
Sierra blue
hammer mill
is the meanest
son of a
biscuit eater
I've ever
fed before'

NADINE

Inside
the natural
skylight
refraction
I studied
Nadine's
tabby pattern

It's no wonder
she's the
smoothest
shapeshifter
I've ever
seen

A streamline
feline...
stretched out
like a
limousine

She's
the only
black cat
to ever
hear her
name

mentioned
eight times
in a hit
Chuck Berry
song

N' don't
get me
wrong –
I always
knew she
was cool –

But when
God painted
her bitchin'
ghost flames

He was
just takin'
this ole
hound
to school

BELLE FOURCHE BLUES

We

were

seventeen

miles

Southwest

of

Sundance

Wyoming

when

the

call

came

in

And

I

knew

then

if

I

was

gonna

be

forced

to

kill

again

That
Four
Corners
in
Weston
County
would
be
as
good
a
place
as
any

To
do
the
job
clean
n'
quick
so
I
could
just
slip
off
in
those

hungy
Bear
Lodge
Mountains

N'
escape
down
the
goddamn
Belle
Fourche
River
like
so
many
years
before

WHITEHORSE WITH WHITEY

We
were
sippin'
Whitehorse
whisky
with
Whitey

The
night
he
told
us
about
Lefty

And
how
much
it's
hurt
him

Every
day
since
that
stroke
took
him

back
in
75

N'
Whitey
says
hardly
a
day
goes
by

Without
hearin'
'That's The Way
Love Goes' –

Then
havin'
to
pull
his
red
Silverado
over
on

the
shoulder
to
cry

HELL TO PAY

I
remember
drivin'
without
headlights
down
old
number
eight

Already
a
few
hours
late
for
my
midnight
curfew

Crankin'
'Way Cool Jr.'
for
the
sixteenth
time

Just
slow
sippin'
a
little
Boone's
Farm
Wine

With
sex
n'
poetry
on
my
hillbilly
mind
And
tan
skin
glistenin'
from
her
sweat
infused
Hawaiian
Tropic
curves

Knowin'
with
damn
few
words
later
that
mornin'
there'd
surely
be
hell
to
pay

PEMISCOT COUNTY

I remember
runnin' guns
Southbound
on 55
In a
raven black
Ford Econoline

Listenin' to
'You Don't
Mess Around
With Jim' –

Over n' over
and over
again –

Never
really knowin'
who'd be
waitin'
on the
other end
Not exactly
achin' to die
in goddamn
Pemiscot County

Like
the night
they clipped
ole Slim
at Cottonwood
Point
Then fed
his cranked
up corpse
to those
flaked out
flatheads
spawnin'
in Big Blue

PEPTO PETE

In the
mid 80s
Pepto Pete
made more
fuck you
money
down in
Tulum
than any
other hitman
from the
Midwest
could
possibly
spend
over three
lifetimes

And
I'll never
forget
the final
words
I offered...
before lettin'
his conscience
bleed –

I said –

'Take a seat...
Pepto Pete
This'll be over
before ya
know it'

MOUND BAYOU

The lanky
State Trooper
just stood
there
on the
driver's side
of my
88 Sedan
DeVille

Shinin' his
8 cell
Mag-Lite
into my
Percocet
primed
pinpoint
pupils

He
wanted
to know
why our
country
asses
were
trollin'
around

Mound Bayou
at a quarter
past two
in the
mornin'

He said –

'This'll be
your only
goddamn
warnin' –

Because
you Yankee
sons-a-bitches
sure as hell
ain't welcome
here in
Mississippi'

MISSIN'

In rural
Missouri
a man
can go
missin'
without
anyone
knowin'
he's gone
for good

Like
those two
cattle buyin'
brothers
from Bondual
Wisconsin

That just
up n'
vanished
last Sunday
mornin'

With
no sign
of a
violent crime
or struggle

Leavin'
dozens
of local
lawmen
puzzled

When
they found
those boys
tricked out
Chevy rental

With it's
diesel engine
still grindin'

In a
commuter lot
almost
40 miles away
from where
they were
last seen
alive

BARRY COUNTY BLUES

In the
mid 90s
I made
a damn
good livin'
buryin'
worthless
sons-a-bitches
in rural
Barry County

N' at
the time
was
absolutely
convinced
my days
were
numbered

So
I never
really planned
on carryin'
all those
grizzly ass
images

around for
twenty four
more years

Hell -
I was still
wet behind
the ears
and just
beggin'
for a
bullet
to come
from one
of those
high end
assassins
that never
found me

BETTER WITH LESS

I could
hear
Mike
Ness
singin'
'Reach
for the
Sky'

That
4th of
July –

The
same
night
Barry
White
died –

As I
tried to
do better
with less
than any
hustler
should

JJ BROTHERS

The
sketchiest
little
tavern
on
South
13th
street
is
JJ
Brothers

It's
cash
only
n'
seldom
closes

I
go
there
after
my
last
night
shift

for
the
week
is
over

To
have
a
few
frosty
Old
Style
pints

And
two
Pistol
Pete's
Polish
sausage
with
spicy
brown
mustard
n'
kraut

CARLO

Carlo carried
an obscene
amount
of money
anytime
we were
sent South
on business

And while
I was still
too green
to do more
than act
as a
witness

I knew
Carlo
used
the skim
whenever
he needed
to pay
for things

we couldn't

come by

fast enough

here in

Kansas

City

ITALIAN BOOGEYMAN

A few
years before
we became
Navy Corpsmen
my friend
Toth got
tangled up
as a paid
DEA
informant

He said
the Feds
suggested
he join
the service
after the
Balistrieri
Brothers
were caught
on tap
talkin' to
'Blue Eyes'
from
Brookfield

Askin' him
to plant
an Italian
boogeyman
in the
backseat
of Toth's
brand new
calypso green
Mustang GT

DOGTOWN

He was
just sittin'
there alone
in the
Florida
room

In his
grandfather's
green
ladderback
chair

Readin'
'A Feast
Of Snakes'
for the
thirteenth
time

Slow sippin'
Blood Oath
from a
Norlan Rauk
heavy rummer

Thinkin'
bout
ole Joe
Strummer's
undiagnosed
heart murmur

Knowin'
his final trip
to Dogtown
was just a
few short
days away

THIMBLEFUL

There's
a thimbleful
of Jacob
Beam's
first batch
Still
clingin'
to the
bottom
in this
hammered
silver
hip flask

And
if I was
a little less
sentimental -
I'd kill
all that's
left...
plain
n' simple –

Before
fillin' it
back

to the

cap

with

Double

Eagle

As

the Devil

makes

more than

empty

promises...

along

Happy

Hollow

Road

TURF WAR

We
would
sit n' sip
St. Ides
every
Saturday
night
on our
North Park
balcony

Just
listenin'
to the
turf war roar
along those
blood soaked
side streets
out in
El Cajon

Knowin'
all the
green ER
nurses
from
Grossmont

would be
belly up
to the bar
at Pete's
Place
after their
shift was
over

Talkin' shop
with all the
off duty cops
about suckin'
chest wounds

n' just
how much
goddamn
damage
a 9mm
hollow point
can do to
vital organs

EZ8 MOTEL

(For Stretch)

When
housekeeping
discovered his
lifeless body
in room 120
at the EZ8
Motel

The
Sunday
paper
was still
untouched
next to
an overflowin'
ashtray
filled with
Winston
100s

And a
fifth of
Old Crow
he'd drained
after his
final show

at the
Silver Fox
Starlite
Lounge
in Bakersfield –

Ole Stretch
always said
he'd just
put one
in his
own
head

Instead of
dyin' slow
the way
his Daddy
did

Strugglin'
too hard
to breathe
with that
goddamn
COPD

And a
stack of
hit songs

nobody
was willin'
to pay
to hear
him play
anymore

AUGUST BLUES

I hear
hints
of the
August
blues
on our
six o'clock
news

As the
heat index
continues
to soar
here in
Kansas
City –

We're
kinda like
a crippled ole
turkey vulture
that's grown
too weak
to circle
all those
rotting
flood claimed

carcasses
along I-29
North of
Saint Joe –

So...
there's
really no need
to waterboard
our whiskey drunk
weatherman
anymore

Because his
hooched
up ass
is wrong

more than
half the time
and this
killin' season
will surely
die on
the vine
sometime
between
Labor Day
n' Halloween

CROOKED WAYS

There's a
one lane
bridge sign
with seventeen
bullet holes
propped up
against a
salvage yard
Monte Carlo
with its ass
smashed in

And every
now n' then
I'll catch him
standin' inside
that crooked
ole fenceline
where he's likely
still searchin'
for a better way
to explain
just why
he did it

LAST HURRAH

David
Berman
died for
our sins
two days
ago

Now
his book
'Actual Air'
is a #1
bestseller

And
I think
it's tragic
he had
to wait
eighteen
desolate
years
to get
there –

So
I made
a final

decision
in the
shower
this mornin'
that I'm
finished
too

Just three
more complete
collections
scheduled to
be ignored
next year
and Linn County
Leg-Breaker
will mark
my last hurrah -
There'll be
no need for
pomp and
circumstance
or fickle fans
lined up
around the
block to
bid me
a fond
farewell

N'
I hope
they won't
waste
their hard
earned
dough
sendin'
flowers
to my
funeral
shell

So few
willingly
supported
my books
while I
was still
around

And
let the
record
reflect
now –

I was
never
really

writin'
them
for the
mercurial
masses
anyway

WAYWARD WILLIE

Wayward
Willie
knew
exactly
how
it
felt
to
have
his
freedom
stripped
away

And
following
a
hard
fifteen
inside
the
tortured
blue
screams
of
Sing
Sing

He
spent
almost
every
afternoon
flat
pickin'
ole
Jimmie
Rodgers
tunes

For
a
captive
audience
of
thirty
six
thousand

At
Cedar
Grove
Cemetery
in
Flushing
Queens

LOCK THE GATE
SAINT PETER

VERSE I

We live
among
the broken
The wild
drunk
n' crooked
Where
everything
is worse
than it
seems –

It's all
paid for
politicians
Feedin'
power hungry
christians
And
no GOD
can save us
at this
speed –

CHORUS-

Saint Peter
lock the gate
tonight
And don't
let them
in
They say
they come
in peace...
despite
Their death
defying
grins
There's no
rest for
the weary
When evil
always
wins
So lock
the gate
Saint Peter
And
don't
let them
in –

Yeah...
lock the gate
Saint Peter
N' don't
let'em
in

VERSE II

We live
like we've
forgotten
Down to
the core
we're rotten
With
no one
to blame
but our
empty
shells –

There's
fresh blood
on the
Bible
Where
selfish

trumps

survival

And

greed is

the only

currency

in hell

REPEAT CHORUS (Twice)

DANGEROUS MAN

A man
is much more
dangerous
when he's
no longer
afraid to
die

Like
there's
a safety
switch
that's been
flipped
somewhere
down deep
in his
insides

Where
guilt got
stacked
like firewood
on a cold
November
night

And
no matter
how many
more
young
assassins
they send

He
plans
to take
a few
of the
most
fearful
back
to hell
with him

COBALT BLUE PENUMBRA

As
wide-eyed
onlookers
stumble over
eggshells

I hear
a fresh-faced
churchgoin'
lady say' –

'Desperate men
do desperate things' –

And it
makes me
wonder
just how
in the hell
she knows

My
brand of
hopelessness
has always
been on
its own

Like clingin'
to the
frayed
end
of a
gallows
rope

Where
all that's
ever mattered
comes to
a sudden
halt
And
unbridled
recklessness
gets stripped
down
to the
neck-bones

As
both boots
swing free
inside a
cracked
cobalt blue
Penumbra

SUBTERRANEAN SHOVEL

In this
virtual world
we're livin'
in

There's
a boneyard
reserved
for fake
family
n' friends

You know –

All those
insecure
pseudo-supporters

The
brand born
to spew
mindless
shit in
dim lit
empty
rooms

Because
they fear
you'll be more
successful
than them
in the
short run

Never
mind
all the
times
you laid
it all
on the
goddamn
line
For every
other clinger
that wanted
somethin'
for nothin'
but got the
subterranean
shovel
instead

DEVIL'S DYKE ROAD

Cotton
Hicks
used to
say –

'It's better
to dance
with the one
that brung
ya
Than
gamble away
your entire
bank roll
Chasin'
rainbows
down
Devil's
Dyke
Road'

CHASE CLUB

We
were
drinkin'
dirty
Grey
Goose
martinis
at
the
Chase
Club
in
Saint
Louis
when
'Shotgun
Vinny'
strolled
through

He
was
wearin'
a
sharply
tailored
Brioni

pinstripe
suit
and
pair
of
Salvatore
Ferragamo
alligator
shoes

And
there
were
two
big
Italian
dudes
flankin'
him
Ya
know-

Just
the
kind
of
gangsters
ya
never
wanna

see
knockin'
through
your
peephole
at
3AM

LIGHTNIN' ON THE PRAIRIE

VERSE I

Where the
switchgrass
waves
my blood
runs cold
Doin'
20
to life
at 46
years
old –

It's a
pawnshop
pistol
on a
whorehouse
rat
Sippin'
Four Roses
Bourbon
from a
little brown
sack –

Yeah -

Four Roses
Bourbon...
from that
little brown
sack

CHORUS -
There's lightnin'
on the prairie
and hurt in
my heart
These
lawbreakin' ways
done tore me
apart -
Still wrecked
most mornin's
when that
ole rooster
crows
Shootin' things
in my veins...
Snortin' smash
up my nose –

Yeah -
things
in my veins...
N' smash
up my
nose

VERSE II

Where
truth got
butchered
on the
slaughterhouse
stairs
My finger
on the trigger
with tallow
in my hair

Like a
bluetick hound
on a full moon
night
Been hoofin'
through
the timber
by minin'
light

Just
a hoofin'
through
the timber
by minin'
light

REPEAT CHORUS (Twice)

THOMAS HILL

VERSE I

Well I
grew up fast
runnin' guns
n' smokin'
weed
Chasin'
hillbilly women
that we're
faster than
me

It was
Uncle Dick's
Terry
with that
big Merc
cruiser
Popin' cold
Silver Bullets
from his
bright green
cooler

CHORUS –

My Mama
said son
you're
bound
to get
killed
Doin'
whatcha
doin...
out on
Thomas Hill

Yeah
doin'
whatcha
doin'...
out on
Thomas Hill

VERSE II

Well I
damn near
drown
on a
blue moon
night
With our
pontoon
anchored

beyond

Mac's Cove

lights

We were

listenin'

to Skynyrd

n' sippin'

Wild Irish

Rose

Just crappie

rig fishin'

where the

warm water

flows

REPEAT CHORUS –

VERSE III

Jim Renner's

Airstream

was up on

blocks

N' ole

Hawaiian

Tropic Heidi

was smokin'

hot

We had
a knock off
Willie...
singin'
'Stay All Night'

And a
Budweiser
truck
with that
red bowtie

REPEAT CHORUS (Twice)

SHE DON'T LOVE ME

VERSE I

There were
hints of
her perfume
on my red
flannel shirt
Sticky smoke
in my lungs
doin' things
to my hurt –

Now
two less
leaves
cause this
orange
burns slow
Mixin'
bourbon
with beer
near the
campfire
glow

Yeah-
Bourbon
with beer

near the
campfire
glow

CHORUS –

I was lost
last night
like a sailor
without
the sea
Still wantin'
her back
but she don't
love me -
Oh I want
her back
but she don't
love me

VERSE II

There were
white flames
dancin'
shootin'
sparks
sky high
Just
listenin'

to Petty
play the
blues
while I
cried –

As the
coyotes
answered
I prayed
they would
come
But
mornin'
came early
n' I still
feel numb

Yeah-
this mornin'
came early
n' I still
feel numb

REPEAT CHORUS (Twice)

TEN DAY DRUNK

I
went
on
a
ten
day
drunk
once
Just
to
see
how
long
it
would
take
for
them
to
come
lookin'

And
fortunately
no
one
thought

to

hunt

for

me

down

in

Waco

Where

I

spent

almost

every

afternoon

sippin'

BIG

Os

at

George's

While

tryin'

to

decide

if

I

really

wanted

to

die

Instead
of
makin'
that
long...
lonely
ass
drive
back
to
Kansas
City

NOBODY REMEMBERS
THE GODDAMN PRETENDERS

Hank
called me
from his
grave
tonight
to say
it's not
fuckin'
worth
it

To just
throw
in the
towel
already
n' find
somethin'
more
meaningful
to do
with what
little time
I have
left

Then
we both
laughed
our flat
asses off
because
real writers
don't have
that kind
of freedom

He said
he was
addicted
to everything
the wannabes
suggested
he shouldn't
do
Hustlin' hard
But only
when he
wanted to

Because
at some point
we all
end up
worm
food

And nobody
remembers
the goddamn
pretenders
anyway

WHEEL GUN MIKE

The
same
August
night
ole
'Wheel
Gun
Mike'
asked
me
why
I
always
carry
two
.45s

Someone
took
his
goddamn
life
in
that
beautiful
circle
drive

Outside

the

new

home

he'd

built

off

Whisperin'

Oaks

out

in

Buffalo

Grove

Because

he

thought

Berwyn

had

become

too

dangerous

Even

for

a

wise

guy

who'd

made

his
bones
so
long
ago
he
must
have
forgotten
just
how
quick
an
inside
hit
could
find
him

BRENDA AT JOE'S

I used
to go
to Joe's
n' drink
when things
turned bleak
Like that
afternoon
in April
when 'The
Possum'
passed
away

I just
sat there
next to
the Seeburg
jukebox
in back
with a
fat stack
of singles
Chasin'
Guinness
Draught
with

Red Breast
fifteen
until Brenda
cut me off

It was
only a
few months
before
the liver
cancer
returned
and took
her away
from me
too

NO PLACE TO GO

Standin'
here alone
n' bleedin'
out slow
on this
freshly
graded
gravel
road

Somewhere
between
the Cox place
and Sawmill
curve
in rural
Linn
County –

It's where
my ravaged
lungs
were born
to take
their last
gasp

And
deep inside
my weary
mind
there are
hollow point
echoes
of Howlin'
Wolf
singin'
'No place
to go' –

While
I carve
a few
final words
on this

shotgun
splattered
hedge post

With
an ole
brass cap
pocket knife
Big Tom
gifted me...
when I was

still naive
enough
to believe
the Lord
could save
me from
anything –

And Hell
wasn't really
worth worryin'
about...
so long
as I lived
my life
right

Or never
left any
witnesses
alive...
long enough
to testify
against
me

WORD HUSTLERS

Word
hustlers
like me
were never
really born
to find the
finish line

So I'll
keep spendin'
what's left
of my
precious
time

Craftin' these
goddamn
crooked
lines...
that
intermittently
rhyme

Because the
pure poetry
swine...
will never
be fine

With
anyone
blessed
to grind
better than
they do

ADAM'S ANTS

Adam was
the youngest son
of the largest
land owner
in Northwest
Nodaway
County
And after
his Dad
had died
suddenly
of a
hemorrhagic
stroke
during
the soybean
harvest
in 95
He
decided
to buy up
every
abandoned
property
he could
find
for just
pennies on
the dollar-

N' over
a sixteen
month span
had acquired
twenty-three
undervalued
homes from
St. Joe
North to
Skidmore
Not to
mention
gettin' hitched
to a prominent
lawyer's daughter
from Kansas City
who was somehow
conveniently
connected
to the Outfit
up in Chicago –

So it's safe
to say
ole Adam
wasn't limited
to growin'
row crops
anymore

Hell
he'd even
painted
every one
of his
meth house
front doors
a bold ass
radish red –

N' said
it wasn't
in an
effort to
thumb his
nose at
all those
Feds
circlin' like
hungry
buzzards
outside
In fact
during their
peak production
in the late 90s...
Adam's ants
were generatin'
just shy
of 4 million

dollars
a day –

Which
made it
too goddamn
easy to pay
all those
crooked
good guys
to stay
away
N' pad
the pockets
of at least
a dozen
legitimate
local business
owners...

Where they'd
clean his cash

So he could stash...
a cool six billion

Before makin'
his grand escape

During plantin'

season...
in the late
rain soaked
Spring of
2003

LOUISE CLIFF

Louise
Cliff
would
just sit
there
in back
at the
First Ward
House

Smokin'
those skinny
brown More
cigarettes

Singin'
along
with every
Ray Charles
song
I'd play
on the
jukebox –

And
it was
red beer

with sea salt
every goddamn
day...
except on
the anniversary
of her
only
daughter's
death

When
she would
slow sip
Seagram's 7
until her
husband Henry
arrived

to take her
car keys
away
just ten
minutes
before
closin' time

DECADES OVERDUE

In this
strange space
we're livin' in
there's no
such thing
as bitter
enemies
or loyal
friends

It's just
an inbred herd
of bloated
egos...
playin'
screw your
neighbor
inside a
burnin' library
with the doors
padlocked shut

And most
starvin' artists
will never
give a fuck...
because

they'd rather
serve to
obstruct
in an effort
to appease
the goddamn
gatekeepers

You know -
all those
self-appointed
rule makers

The ones
that earned
their success
the old
fashioned way
Through
inheritance
or plain ole
pseudo-intellectual
arrogance

I say
we let
the greedy
bastards
burn...

You bring
the marshmallows

N' I'll buy
the beer

We're
already
more than
a few
decades
overdue

WHEN THE WINE

He sipped
Sweet muscadine
From a quart
Canteen
N' tried
Real hard
Not to lie
Bout things –

But time
Twists funny
And makes
Wicked rings
When the wine
Runs short
N' songs
Won't sing –

When the wine
Runs short...
N' songs
Won't sing –

Said he killed
Twelve men
When he was
Only twenty-three

Wearin' German
Uniforms
In those
Hills of Sicily –

Such a heavy
Price to carry
Despite...
Stayin' free
When the wine
Runs short
N' songs
Won't sing –

When the wine
Runs short...
N' songs
Won't sing –

Drove a silver
Continental
N' wore big
Diamond bling
From Saint Louis
To Memphis
Then on
To Hot Springs –

Packed his
War worn Colt

And a haymaker
Swing
When the
Wine ran short
N' songs
Wouldn't sing

Oh -
When the wine
Ran short...
N' songs
Wouldn't sing

SURGEON'S SCALPEL

The
recently
retired
surgeon's
scalpel
is
still
as
sharp
as
it
ever
was

Unfortunately
he's
just
like
the
rest
of
us

Time
finally
found
his

once
long
n'
nimble
now
crippled
fingers

And
cut
them
off
at
their
fuckin'
knees

CLEAN SLATE SMILE

Uncle
Henry
always
had
this
clean
slate
smile
that
looked
like
freshwater
mussel
shells
that
were
washed
ashore
after
a
strong
Summer
thunderstorm
on
Moonshine
Beach

COFFEE WITH CHESTER

In
September
of
2003
we
took
Ricky's
ivy
green
Road
Runner
from
Rutledge
North
to
Racine

Then
met
Chester
Commodore
for
French
press
coffee
in
the

General
Grant
Suite
at
Maxwell
Mansion
off
Baker
Street
in
Lake
Geneva

LOAN SHARK FROM BOLINAS

I met
an old
loan shark
from Bolinas
at the
Siren Canteen
on Stinson Beach

He was
perusing
Seven Watermelon Suns
(No. 1)...

Sipping fresh
carrot juice
mixed with
Calvados

And said
he had enough
'Trout Money'
to buy forty
Pine Creek acres
twice
in the

next life

if his

fifth wife

would

agree

HUNDREDS OF MILES
AWAY FROM HOME

While
I
sip
this
scorched
breakfast
blend
from
the
truck
stop
styrofoam
I
poured
it
in

I
wonder
if
the
skinny
lot
lizards
make
time

and
a
half
on
Saturdays
too

As
I
try
n'
dissect
all
the
twisted
things
lonely
men
do
when
we're
still
hundreds
of
miles
away
from
home

RIVERBOAT ROULETTE

There was
an eighteen
month stretch
when riverboat
roulette
was the
only thing
I had left
to hang
onto

I was so
addicted
to that
goddamn
rhythmic
click...

I woulda
sold my
sorry soul
away
for a
fat stack
hit on
the red
fourteen

TRACIE INSTEAD

We were
fallin' out
of love
faster than
two flat tires
in a short story
penned by
Larry Brown

And every
swingin' dick
in our little
Bible belt
one-horse
town
could see it
except me

Because
I'd just
turned
sixteen
n' saved
my farmhand
scratch
to buy
her a

second hand
promise ring

Infatuated
with all the
impossibilities
and too
goddamn green
to accept
she was
way outta
my league

I would
never be
fast or
fuckin'
tough
enough
to catch

let alone
keep her

And if
I had only
known
how bad
I was bound
to hurt

on the
dead end
of that
goodbye
dial tone

I might
have spent
more time
chasin'
her best
friend
Tracie
instead

ROUNDHOUSE RICK

Three hours before
my Uncle Cecil
introduced me to
Roundhouse Rick
for the first time

I had noticed
his grabber green
Maverick
parked behind
the Moberly
Brick Plant

He was doin'
one-armed
push-ups
over a
big breasted
cashier
from Bratcher's
market

And still had
her cherry red
lipstick
inside the
diagonal

crease
of his
cauliflower ear
when he
reached out
to shake my
hand that
warm Autumn
afternoon

PLATINUM BLONDE BARMAID

When
the
platinum
blonde
barmaid
from
Felix
Street
Pub
suddenly
fell
in
love
with
the
bartender's
older
brother

We
all
knew
his
ass
was
screwed
because

she

kept

a

long

twisted

list

of

younger

lovers...

that

ole

widowed

son

of

a

bitch

would

have

to

contend

with

And

it

was

gonna

be

damn

near

impossible

for

a

rural

letter

carrier

from

Ravenwood

to

play

the

sucker

long

enough

so

hers

would

look

like

an

accident

too

NO ORDINARY BEGGAR

I made
eye contact
with a
desperate man
this afternoon
at the
intersection
of I-70
and 7 HWY

He was holdin'
a rain soaked
cardboard sign
that said -

'Diagnosed
with cancer
in March...

Lost my
Union job
in June...

And
can't even
afford to
die with

dignity
anymore'

So I
pulled
my car
over
on the
shoulder
and put
the flashers
on

Rolled my
window down
and gave him
all the cash
I had on me

And when
he mentioned
this was
the most
difficult
thing
he never
dreamed
he'd be
forced
to do
I shook

that man's
tremblin'
hand
and said -

'None of us
have any idea
what the
future holds

N' while
I don't
have a clue
specifically
what you're
goin' through

I do
understand
how vulnerable
we all are

And
just
wanted
you to
know

I
believe
you'

GODDAMN GUTTERS GURGLE

As
I
listen
to
the
goddamn
gutters
gurgle

I
watch
this
middle-
aged
weatherman
on
Channel
5

Movin'
his
arms
around
like
a
Pentecostal
preacher

Never
knowin'
why
I've
decided
to
mute
him
again

WARMEST REGARDS

When
Chain
Smokin'
Charlie
pulled
that
quart
size
Ziploc
bag
of
liberty
caps
from
the
left
breast
pocket
of
his
red
Brioni
blazer

He
said –

'Trickshot

Tommy

sends

his

warmest

regards

from

the

Highlands

in

Carmel-

by-

the-

Sea'

TEN HIGH TOM

We
were
layin'
low
at
Bayou
on
the
Vine –

Sippin'
Stag's
Leap
Cask
23 –

When
Ten
High
Tom
told
us
he'd
been
diagnosed
with
Stage

IV
pancreatic
cancer –

It
was
just
six
days
prior
to
his
youngest
daughter's
wedding
in
Jamaica –

And
somehow
I
knew
ole
Tom
would
be
gone
weeks
before
the

Snake
Parade
on
St.
Patrick's
Day

SAWTOOTH BENDS

Where
in
the
hell
did
this
all
begin

I
know
better
now
since
ya
ain't
my
friend

Like
gravel
dust
ridin'
a
forgotten
wind
Just
skeletal
remains

with
them
sawtooth
bends

Where
nowhere
bound…
only
means
the
end

It's
just
gravel
dust
flyin'
n'
them
sawtooth
bends

Yeah –
gravel
dust
flyin'…

N'
them
sawtooth
bends

IF I HAD A PILL

If
I had
a pill
for every
phantom hill
taken...
heart still
breakin'...
n' dirty hand
I've shaken

I could fill
a wholesale
warehouse
twice the size
of my
fancy ass
mail order
pharmacy
out in
Phoenix

Yeah-
If
I had
a pill
for every time

some sick
son of a bitch
threatened
to kill
me or
my family

Or turn
my somewhat
sketchy activities
into the
city...state
n' federal
authorities

I could
fill every
goddamn
prison cell
in the
Midwest
and have enough
refills left
to sell them
back to you
at three times
their current
street value

Oh -
If
I had
a pill
for every
hole I have
left to fill...
soul I'm
bound to
steal...
and truth
too raw
to feel

I could
drill screws
through your
tired skull...
n' never
wake you
at all
because
the half-life
of your
illegitimate
actions
just expired

MEEKS FAMILY MURDER

When

Governor

Stone

pardoned

Gus

Meeks

in

April

of

1894

he

had

no

idea

what

George

and

William

Taylor

were

capable

of

Ya

see...

Ole

Gus

was

a

tenant

farmer

on

Linn

County

land

owned

by

the

Taylors

and

pled

guilty

as

a

favor

when

implicated

in

one

of

their

cattle

rustlin'

schemes

But
when
he
refused
to
take
a
thousand
dollars
n'
disappear
upon
release
from
the
penitentiary

The
Taylors
just
shot
him...

His
pregnant
wife...

And
four
year

old
daughter

Then
attempted
to
beat
two
other
daughters
to
death
with
a
rock

Leavin'
little
Nelli
barely
clingin'
to
life
in
a
shallow
family
grave
covered
with

hay
that
was
too
damp
to
catch
fire

And
she
served
as
sole
witness
when
the
pair
were
finally
sentenced
to
hang
in
April
of
1896

But...
evil

has

a

twisted

mind

of

its

own

sometimes

and

when

the

Taylors

broke

out

of

their

holdin'

cell

in

Kansas

City

just

nineteen

days

before

execution

Only

William

would

pay
the
ultimate
price
after
being
captured
twice
because
George
was
never
seen
or
heard
from
again

HAIR-TRIGGER

Jim
spent
nearly
half
his
life
in
cell
No.
66
at
Stillwater
State
Prison

After
he
n'
his
brothers
got
shot
up
during
that
botched
bank

job
up
in
Northfield

And
when
they
were
finally
paroled
in
1901...
Jim
couldn't
wait
to
get
his
hands

on
another
Smith
and
Wesson

So
he
could

end
things
clean
n'
quick...
never
dreamin'
it
would
take
several
hours
to
slip
away
after
pullin'
the
goddamn
hair-
trigger
himself

BIG BEER CAN HILL

We
chased
the
fading
tail
lights
in
Toth's
midnight
blue
Toronado

Until
they
finally
shook
us

Somewhere
between
Session's
liquor
store
and
Wilburn's
service
station

Just
six
miles
East
of
Meadville

On
big
beer
can
hill

SHADE LESS THAN SOBER

On
the
shade
less
than
sober
October
night
Sheriff
O'Dell
pulled
me
over

I
was
wheelin'
n'
dealin'
in
Mom's
Delta
88

Just
listenin'
to

Ozzy
on
bootleg
tape

Tryin'
hard
to
remember
the
alphabet
backwards

Knowin'
full
well

he'd
haul
my
sorry
ass
to
jail

If
I
so
much
as

mentioned
takin'
that
ole
'Crazy
Train'
on
home

THE LAST LIGHT IS LEAVIN'

The
last
light
is
leavin'...
now
almost
gone

Like
Leonard
Cohen
singin'...
a
Hank
Williams
song –

It's
a
sad
Campbell
riff...
since
Petty's
moved
on

Oh -
The
last
light
is
leavin'...
now
almost
gone ---

Yeah -
The
last
light
is
leavin'...
now
almost
gone

You
can
hear
a
snare
fill...
that
hints
of
Levon –

It's
Willie
singin'
Waylon
with
Cash
and
Kristofferson

Oh -
The
last
light
is
leavin'...
now
almost
gone ---

The
last
light
is
leavin'...
now
almost
gone

Like
that
ole

n'

lonsome...

Jimmy

Martin

rode

on –

It's

smoother

than

the

whiskey...

that

took

Whitley

young

Oh -

The

last

light

is

leavin'...

now

almost

gone ---

Yeah -
The
last
light
is
leavin'...
n'
it's
time
to
roll
on

WORTHLESS MEMORIES

I was
listenin' to
Harry Dean
Stanton
carefully recite
'Bluebird' by
Charles Bukowski
on the
same night
my first wife
got tired
of all my
horseshit
n' split
with our
only son –

And the
next mornin'
shortly after
I'd gone
to work
a double
shift –

She had
the Mighty Movers

safely transport
our modest
possessions
back to
Bartlett –

Except
an old
Budweiser box
filled to the brim
with worthless
memories
she didn't
wanna be
reminded of
anymore

WHISKEY SOAKED SOUL

The
paramedics
said
his
speedometer
was
locked
at
a
hundred
n'
ten
when
they
airlifted
what
little
was
left
of
him
from
that
snow
fence
in
Grundy
County –

And
Trooper
Cooper
claimed
during
their
crash
impact
analysis
the
driver
had
been
thrown
through
the
windshield

of
that
Ninety-
Two
Silverado
in
a
manner
unmatched
over
his
thirty

five
years
with
the
Missouri
State
Highway
Patrol –

N'
we
fought
like
hell
to
salvage
his
twisted
and
shattered
shell
that
night –

But
I
knew
as
soon
as

we
hit
his
pupils

with
the
penlight
and
resumed
the
code
that
his
whiskey
soaked
soul
had
already
moved
on

STUNNED SILENT SHADOWS

Somewhere

tonight

I'll

stand

alone

inside

the

stunned

silent

shadows-

Holdin'

your

warm

wrinkled

left

hand

in

mine –

Asking

myself

why

I

would

rather

ride

with
you –

Than
attempt
to
rescue
all
those
cold
sufferin'
souls
I
was
never
meant
to
save

MUDDY WATER

Soakin' some Samuel Clemens
Down by White Earth River
Three lines gettin' wet
While I marinate my liver

Friday fishin's
Been good to me
So why the hell
Change it now

Just soakin' some Samuel Clemens
N' makin' it through somehow

This muddy water calls to me
When I'm all alone
Invitin' my legs to wade on in
N' ease my weary bones

I feel the grief of a thousand years
As an ancient echo moans
The muddy water calls to me
In a voice just like my own

Yeah - this muddy water calls to me
In a voice just like my own
Tryin' a few new lines
In the afternoon shade

Sippin' homemade hootch
From a jug my Grandpa made

Sure do miss that wise man
Sometimes somethin' fierce
Starin' at his pocket watch
N' fightin' back the tears

Yeah- sippin' homemade hootch
N' fightin' back the tears

This muddy water calls to me
When I'm all alone
Invitin' my legs to wade on in
N' ease my weary bones

I feel the grief of a thousand years
As an ancient echo moans
The muddy water calls to me
In a voice just like my own

Oh - the muddy water calls to me
In a voice just like my own

Sprawled out
On this sandbar
Listenin' to
Faron Young
Farm markets
N' local news

A few fish…
Better than none

Yeah- Heifers, Hogs
Bulls n' frogs
A few fish…
Better than none

This muddy water calls to me
When I'm all alone
Invitin' my legs to wade on in
N' ease my weary bones

I feel the grief of a thousand years
As an ancient echo moans
The muddy water calls to me
In a voice just like my own

Oh - the muddy water calls to me
In a voice just like my own

PAPAW

Papaw was singin'
The 'Mule Skinner Blues'
Down at Sammy's
Last Saturday night
And I got
Just a little too edgy...
Feelin' somethin'
Wasn't right ---

When four stormed through
The front door...
I saw the flash
With my own two eyes
Papaw's steady
With that .38
N' only one of
Them survived ---

Yeah -
Papaw's steady
With a .38
Won't flench...
He'll take your life ---

Papaw was pickin'
A pawnshop axe
Down at Sammy's

Last Saturday night
And we got
So stoned on Willie
Chasin' Stardust
With one headlight---

When the law
Walked through the front door
I saw'em motion...
Over Papaw's side
N' that's when he
Let'em have it
With that Tommy
Slingin' .45s

Yeah -
That's when he
Let'em have it
With that Tommy
Slingin' .45s ---

Cause ya just
Don't cross ole Papaw
Won't flench...
He'll take your life

NECK OF THE WOODS

There's evil out
On the high plains
Where gamblin'
Won't do no good
Like a hitcher
In hooptie hell
Or coke runner...
On wheels of wood –

When there ain't
Enough time
To shake those
Demons loose
Even though...
Ya know...
You should

Oh-
There's evil out
On the high plains
And hell in this
Neck of the woods –

Yeah -
There's evil out
On the high plains
N' hell in my
Neck of the woods

HOMICIDE IN HUNTSVILLE

When
KRES
radio
broke
the
news
at
Noon
regarding
a
triple
homicide
down
in
Huntsville –

We'd
already
ditched
our
getaway
car
in
Clifton
Hill –

N'

switched

over

to

Uncle

Frank's

farm

truck

that

was

conveniently

hitched

to

a

gooseneck

loaded

with

Yorkshire

hogs -

Because

no

one

in

rural

Randolph

County

would

ever

expect

a

hillbilly
hit
squad
rollin'
North
on
Route
3
in
middle
of
the
afternoon

DEADEYE DAVE

Deadeye
Dave
chose
to
save
all
of
his
spent
brass
from
contracts
in
a
Dinty
Moore
beef
stew
can –

And
always
said
killin’
folks
for
the

sake
of
money
alone
was
all
he'd
ever
known –

And
I'm
goddamn
certain
when
I
slung
back

that
moldy
ass
shower
curtain –

Ole
Dave
shit
himself
sideways

when

he

realized

I

was

the

friend

they

decided

to

send

to

end

it

UNPREDICTABLE

As
I
study
her
crooked
frown
through
the
lighter
flame
flicker –

My
eyes
swing
dance
inside
the
sensual
silver
smoke
escaping
her
Ruby
Woo
lips –

Oh -

she's

gonna

grind

those

Bessie

Smith

hips

to

the

raw

rhythm

of

Wynonie

Harris –

While

a

seventh

Benson

&

Hedges

smolders

in

the

juke

joint

ashtray –

And
I'll
try
n'
find
somethin'
smooth
to
say –

Before
the
band
takes
its
final
break
or
I've
had
way
too
many
doubles
to
drink –

And
slink
outside

to

sit

on

my

tailgate

until

the

gravel

dust

dies –

Or

I

sober

up

enough

to

realize

she's

way

too

unpredictable

for

a

gambler

as

good

as

me

GRAVEYARD BONES

Some days
I wanna smoke
'Lucky Strikes'
On others…
I'll roll my own

And at 2 AM…
When I have no friends
I prefer…
To ride alone –

There's mornin's
Before
The ole Sun
Wakes up

When you
Can bet
My ass…
Is still
Stoned -

Oh-
Some days
It's all
'Amazing Grace'

On others…

I'm rollin'
Graveyard
Bones

Yeah –
Some days
It's all
'Amazing Grace'

On others….

I'm rollin'
Graveyard
Bones --

Some nights
I like to ramble
On others…
I'll drink
Alone

And at 3AM…
I don't need fake friends
I'd much rather
Hide at home -

Cause there's
Evenin's before
The ole Moon
Wakes up

When you
Can bet
My ass...
Is still
Stoned -

Oh –
Some days
It's all
'Amazing Grace'

On others...

I'm rollin'
Graveyard
Bones

Yeah-
Some days
It's all
'Amazing Grace'

On others...

I'm rollin'
Graveyard
Bones

DEATH THROES

I'm
neck
deep
in
the
death
throes –

Listenin'
to
my
dyslexic
heart
skip
slow –

While
hungover
hellhounds
chase
my
crooked
ass
soul
across
Medicine
Creek –

And
there's
really
never
enough
time
for
a
hungry
hustler
like
me
to
eat-

Or
feel
fulfilled
with
any
goddamn
choice
for
a
last
meal-

Let
alone
this

ragged...
rigged
n'
rotten
roulette
wheel –

Stealthily
determined
to
burn
through
another
fat
stack
of
stolen
scratch –

That's
been
ridin'
high
on
the
red
fourteen –

While
I

sit

n'

watch

in

disbelief -

As

all

my

wet

dreams

evaporate

faster

than

an

aged

single

malt

on

Sunday –

Or

blood

spatter

on

pay

gravel –

With

a

gold

tooth
grin
that
only
the
devil
can
read

NO BETTER TIME FOR THE BLUES

In the midst
of cripplin'
chaos
there's no
better time
for the
blues ---

You
know -
Those
deep
South...
Cottonmouth...
Shootin'
the
goddamn
pole
lights
out
kinda
blues ---

The
pawnshop
Smith
with

its
last
few
digits
spent –

Like
all
those
long
shots
I
shoulda
sent –

Before
Slim
got
grazed
on
stage
down
in
Montgomery ---

You
know -
Those
razor
thin

skinny

sons-

a-

bitches-

The

ones

with

constant

tweaker

twitches -

The

kind

they

find

floatin'

in

backwoods

bar

ditches ----

Yeah-

In the midst

of cripplin'

chaos

there's no

better time

for the

blues ---

You
know –

Those
bacon
grease
poppin'..
Stetson
lid
cockin'...
Fancy
name
droppin'
brand
of
the
blues ---

N'
I'm
almost
ready
to
duel
with
death
again...

Are
you?

BLOODY NOSE RIDGE

When
I
met
Ted
at
the
Brown
Bear
on
Memorial
Day
in
99 –

He
was
sippin'
White
Horse
n'
half
listenin'
to
Linda
bitch
about
her

4th D I V O R C E –

Ted
said
he'd
gone
on
n'
planned
his
own
goddamn
funeral –

Since
he
still
couldn't
tell
his
kids
about
all
those
horrible
things
he
did
up

on
Bloody
Nose
Ridge
back
in
44 –

Then
his
voice
cracked
a
little
more
n'
he
said ---

'It was worse
than war
on Peleliu

Made six days
in September
feel like
five lifetimes
wrapped inside
a riddle

If sad
twin fiddles
could play
the Type 92
machine gun
blues'

WELL INTENTIONED

On
the
nights
I
do
what
feels
right
I'm
wrong
at
least
half
the
time –

And
it's
not
like
I'm
tryin'
to
hide
some
sophisticated
crime –

Or
pay
twice
the
price
for
sins
I'm
bound
to
commit
again
in
my
next
life –

Oh -
there'll
be
no
mention
concernin'
my
perpetual
lack
of
attention
or
well

intentioned

escape

from

this

self-

imposed

prison-

Nevermind

partisan

politics...

Organized

religion...

Or

that

high-

tone

woman

standin'

bare

ass

naked

in

our

Summer

kitchen –

Cookin'

hickory

smoked

bacon

with

eggs

over-

easy

most

Sunday

mornin's

around

3AM

NO MERCY FOR A MURDERER

When
we
were
sent
to
meet
Dallas
down
in
Waco –

He'd
already
done
just
a
shade
less
than
a
decade
in
the
Missouri
State
pen-

And
by
then
he'd
been
a
fugitive
from
justice
for
a
few
months
or
so-

He
was
still
facin'

five
life
sentences
and
need
us
to
help

him
flee
the
country –

But
there
would
be
no
mercy
for
a
murderer
that
day
at
Billy's
Ice
House –

Cause
when
'Johnny
Joe'
decided
someone
needed
to
go –

There
wasn't
gonna
be
another
goddamn
stay
of
execution

DOUBLE DEUCES

My
steel
is
stainless
and
I'm
way
more
dangerous
than
any
MAGA
hat
wearin'
asshole –

Spewin'
senseless
shit
over
Ted's
barber
shop
radio –

Steady
peacockin'

n'
name
droppin'
like
some
impotent
sideshow
dynamo –

Who's
been
chained
to
the
same
ole
glory
hole -
He's
been
workin'
since
the
last
goddamn
straw
poll-

While
buildings
burn...

As
our
World
turns –

And
death
deals
double
deuces...

At
the
Greektown
up
in
Detroit

POWER OF WE

I'm standin'
here alone
in our sparse
front yard
off Sunview –

Holdin' a
fluorescent green
garden hose –

Waterin' patches
of freshly sown
bluegrass –

As an
unmarked cruiser
circles through
the cul-de-sac –

And it makes
me wonder
just how many
men like me –

Are stewin'
over what
they witnessed

happen to
George Floyd
this week –

Knowin'
I'll celebrate 47
next Sunday –

While his
fractured family
struggles to
breathe –

Inside an
impossible grief
that didn't have
to be –

Which
reminds me...

How tragedy
can sometimes fuel
monumental change –

If enough
folks believe
in the power
of we –

And speak
collectively...

Coherently...

Unselfishly...

Together

EVILDOERS EXIT UGLY

As
a
Registered
Nurse
I've
witnessed
evildoers
exit
ugly
hundreds
of
times –

Their
withered
shells
sufferin'
n'
bargainin'
late
into
the
night –

Beggin'
for
better

painkillers
to
help
them
die
more
peacefully –

Unfortunately
they
tend
to
linger
a
little
longer –

Attemptin'
to
reconcile
all
the
wicked
shit
they've
slung –

Their
sunken
n'

guilty
eyes
never
really
seem
too
surprised –

They
remind
me
of
all
those
gutless
gunslingers –

Knees
shakin'
while
standin'
on
the
gallows
trapdoor –

As
an
eager
executioner
smirks...

Just
seconds
before
everything
fades
back
to
black

PERPETUAL IGNORANCE

(For Shep)

Shep
was
just
sittin'
on
the
side
stoop
at
Belle
Tavern –

Sippin'
on
some
of
that
homemade
muscadine
wine –

His
half
brother
Devine
had
bootlegged

outta
Blytheville –

And
I
remember
the
Cards
were
up
three
on
the
Cubs
after
eight –

When
Shep
shut
the
lid
on
his
custom
gator
belly
dreadnought
case –
N'
said...

Medgar
was murdered
30 years ago
today...

And ain't
a goddamn
thing changed –

Except
the price
of shine
on Sundays...

N' all these
sketchy ass
sheet wearin'
sons-of- bitches...

Preachin'
bout needin'
the Lord's
everlasting
forgiveness –

While the
roots of
perpetual
ignorance
remains
the same'

ON SOUTH TO WACO

Tonight
I
feel
like
the
shattered
right
headlight
in
that
nocturne
blue
442
we
boosted
from
Gearhead
Auto
Sales
down
in
Joplin –

It
was
the
same

night
Chris
Farley
died
and
we'd
decided
to
take
a
little
joy
ride
over
to
The
Body
Shop
in
Miami –

I
knew
we
needed
some
more
stash
n'
wanted

to
watch
those
long
legged
peelers
prance –

Before
hittin'
the
drawers
at
Welch
State
Bank
and
makin'
our
way
on
South
to
Waco

APOLOGIES

Apologies to you
And those I've hurt

Like crooked lines left
In the whispering dirt

It's everything I wanted
Then nothin' at all

Just satin beach glass
On a cliff drive wall –

I'm a rusted out fender
In the mid mornin' rain

And a last twelve pack
On an old freight train

There's thunder in the rails
Where nothin' good grows

N' you can hear Hank Williams
Oh…'My Heart Would Know'

Yeah- you can hear ole Hank
N' 'My Heart Would Know' –

Apologies to you
For all the lies I told

Rollin' snake eye dice
Just cheatin' my soul

I'm a selfish…sad bastard
With nothin' to lose

And an empty shell pickin'
Those wanderin' blues –

I'm ditchwater high
In this riverbank mud

Just wettin' a line
N' feelin' unloved

Gone heartsick lonesome
Like a steel guitar

Feelin' bygone guilty
N' graveyard tired

Yeah – I'm bygone guilty
N' graveyard tired

LITTLE ROCK LUTHER

There's a nickel Smith
Ridin' on his dash
With a Velvet can
Chock-full o' cash

An old redbone hound
In his passenger seat
While Burnside grinds
He'll stomp those feet –

Little Rock Luther
Sells Muscadine wine
Outta the trunk
Of his Sixty-Nine...

Ole Little Rock Luther
Sure knows what's good
Up here in this city
Or back in them woods ---

There's a fat stack o' vinyl
In his Falstaff crate
Sellin'...three for ten
Or two for eight

Ain't nobody dicker
N' best bring cash

Cause ya know ole Luther
Don't take no sass –

Little Rock Luther
Sells Muscadine wine
Outta the trunk
Of his Sixty-Nine...

Ole Little Rock Luther
Sure knows what's good
Up here in this city
Or back in them woods –

There's five in the chamber
With four on the floor
And Bondo ripple...
N' waves galore

Claims he ran with Otis
Before his bird went down
And swears the Bar-Kays
Were best around --
Little Rock Luther
Sells Muscadine wine
Outta the trunk
Of his Sixty-Nine...

Ole Little Rock Luther
Sure knows what's good
Up here in this city

Or back in them woods

Yeah -
Little Rock Luther
Sure knows what's good

WHERE THE HOWLER ROAMS

There's an old man perched
On a wrecked coal crane
Says he'll dance all night
For some Hoodoo rain

Those boys from Noyes
Sippin' Show Me shine
Just crooked legs shufflin'
In three quarter time - -

Shaver through the speakers
In a square box Chevy
As ball lightnin' flashes
Cross Atchison levee

Porch bulbs burnin'
But we ain't headed home
Gonna run all night
Where the Howler roams

Yeah...
We'll ride all night
Where the Howler roams - -

There's a salty dog sittin'
With his Sweet Sixteen
Says he'll shoot the damn Moon
If ya know what I mean

Ain't nobody callin'
An ole bootlegger's bluff
We're just hillbilly hustlers...
Doin' this n' such - -

When Shaver tells his story
Bout that 'Ragged Old Truck'
Hail starts bouncin'
As the sky opens up

Porch bulbs burnin'
But we ain't headed home
Gonna run all night
Where the Howler roams

Yeah...
We'll ride all night
Where the Howler roams

Havin' one more
For Shaver...

Where the Howler roams

HOPPER EYES

Hopper eyes...
N' a Madsen smirk
This high plains hitchin'
Is dirty work

Been ridin' the rail
With a Hopi ghost
Hopper eyes...
Watchin' Madsen smoke ---

Taos tremble
N' Trojillo tan
Like turquoise rings
On a writers hand

Southpaw vibrato
Silver claw sharp
Hopper eyes ...
N' Madsen's spark ---

Cocaine karma
On death rattle road
Thousands of pesos
Up a broken nose

Three pistols loaded
Paranoid shakes

Hopper eyes...
Like a rattlesnake ---

No truth in a gambler
All whiskey n' mouth
Deeper than desperate
When the cards play out

Makin' somethin' from nothin'
Ain't nobody's choice
In Hopper's eyes...
Hearin' Madsen's voice –

Purgatory playbill
In lobby card hell
Just a high plains Shakespeare
With a turnpike tell

Faster than cool hand
Gettin' wiser with age
Like Hopper's eyes
N' Madsen's gaze ---
A Kristofferson Sunday
In clean...dirty threads
Cancer stick skinny
Alone in the head

Hooker on the jukebox
In some all night joint
Hawkin' Hopper's eyes
Watchin' Madsen point ---

Ray Ban reflection
Just a hint of chlorine
A sawdust...swing dance
With ole Irene

Lies in motion...
Worn smoother than silk

Hopper eyes...
N' a Madsen tilt

DRAWIN' DEAD

One
of
the
greatest
gifts
I've
ever
received

Was
a
kick
in
the
ass
from
an
old
Marine –

He said –

Son...
don't
ya
dare
end

up
like
me

Drawin'
dead
every
goddamn
Sunday –

Just
twisted
inside
these
blue
collar...
bourbon
soaked
dreams

I
never
had
the
balls
to
chase
or
near
enough
speed

RAZOR THIN

There's a
Razor thin rim
Between the swift
N' the dead

Like lines
Unwritten
Rollin' around
In my head

When hard
Seems so simple
Yet no one
Dare try

And the
Razor thin rim
Just envelopes
The sky ---

There's a
Razor thin edge
Between precious
And fake

Where fools
Get played

More serpent
Than snake

When the lies
Stack up
At least
Skyscraper high

And the
Razor thin edge
Just swallows
The sky ---

There's a
Razor thin margin
Between lucky
And broke

When those
Wall Street pimps
Trick out
Desperate folk
You can watch
The sheep slaughter
If you'll open
Your eyes

As a
Razor thin margin

Slowly

Strangles

The

Sky

BLOODLETTING IN COLCHESTER

We
were
ridin'
the
lightin'
along
136
just
Southeast
of
Vishnu
Springs
when
our
headlights
hit
him ---

He
was
shufflin'
slow
with
a
left
leanin'
switch

engine
limp ---

Wearin'
a
buckshot
ravaged
houndstooth
overcoat
and
Homburg
hat
with
it's
brim
laid
flat ---

N'
when
Spindley
rolled
the
driver's
side
window
down
in
that
souped

up
Delta
88 ---

The
middle
aged
man
said
somethin'
salty...
bout
gettin'
ambushed
over
in
Colchester
just
a
few
hours
prior ---

And
how
those
rotten
ass
sons
of

bitches
best
get
to
hidin' ---

Before
he
could
make
his
way
back
from
Vinegar
Springs
with
Fatty
n'
Chick ---

Because
they'd
surely
bury
all
of
those
worthless
bastards---

Down
deep
in
some
La Moine
River
Valley
gob
pile ---

Where
not
even
they're
own
next
of
kin
could
find'em

KILLIE

Ole
John
Jay
used
to
say
'Killie'
Wagle
would
do
anything
for
ya ---

Unless
you
crossed
him ---

Then
he
might
just
do
anything
to
ya ---

And
Moon
sure
as
hell
knew
more
than
he'd
ever
admit ---

Because
that
Ball
fruit
jar
filled
with
blood
clots
n'
buckshot ---

Had
been
ridin'
high
on
his

weathered

backbar

since

April

of

29

STIRRIN' STICK

My
old
friend
Hal
called
collect
this
mornin' ---

He said –

Son...

Some
extended
time
off
is
usually
damn
good
work
if
you
can
find
it ---

But
between
a
cancer
scare
n'
COVID-19 ---

This
year
can
kiss
my
flat
wrinkled
ass ---

And
when
I
look
back
at
all
those
days
I
wasted
away
worryin' ---

I
know
down
deep
inside
my
shell-
shocked
soul ---

That
there's
bound
to
be
somethin'
better ---

Well
beyond
the
sorry
ole
shit
this
sticks
been
stirrin'

LOUSY GODDAMN FISHERMAN

Shep
used
to
swear
that
a
man
must
be
good
at
least
four
things
during
his
natural
life
span ---

Fightin'...

Fishin'...

Fuckin'...

And
Forgettin' ---

Now...
some
thirty-
six
odd
years
since
I
first
heard
him
say
it ---

One
thing
I
can
concede...

within
ninety
nine
percent
certainty ---

I'm
a
lousy
goddamn
fisherman

Americana songwriter and Kansas-City-based storyteller K.W. Peery is the author of twelve poetry collections. He is founder and editor of *The Angel's Share Literary Magazine*. His work is included in the Vincent Van Gogh Anthology *Resurrection of a Sunflower*, *The Cosmic Lost and Found: An Anthology of Missouri Poets* and *The Konza Poetry Project Presents: Somewhere Between Kansas City And Denver* (Spartan Press). Peery's work has been published in *The Main Street Rag*, *Chiron Review*, *San Pedro River Review*, *The Gasconade Review*, *Big Hammer*, *Blink Ink*, *Rusty Truck*, *Mad Swirl*, *Veterans Voices Magazine*, *Outlaw Poetry*, *Mojave River Review*, *The Asylum Floor*, *Horror Sleaze Trash*, *Ramingo's Porch*, *From Whispers to*

Roars, Fearless Poetry Zine, Culture Cult Magazine, Punk Noir, Mutata Re, The Beatnik Cowboy and *Apache Poetry.* Credited as a lyricist and producer, Peery's work appears on more than twenty studio albums over the past decade.

Website: www.kwpeery.com

CPSIA information can be obtained
at www.ICGtesting.com
Printed in the USA
BVHW071621170921
616961BV00004B/447

9 781952 411687